In the beginning was the Word, and the Word was with God, and the Word was God. . . . And the Word became flesh, and dwelt among us, and we saw His glory, glory as of the only begotten from the Father, full of grace and truth.

JOHN 1:1, 14 NASB

Now all glory to God, who is able to keep you from falling away and will bring you with great joy into his glorious presence without a single fault. All glory to him who alone is God, our Savior through Jesus Christ our Lord. All glory, majesty, power, and authority are his before all time, and in the present, and beyond all time!

JUDE 1:24–25 NLT

Real wisdom, God's wisdom, begins with a holy life and is characterized by getting along with others. It is gentle and reasonable, overflowing with mercy and blessings. . . . You can develop a healthy, robust community that lives right with God and enjoy its results only if you do the hard work of getting along with each other, treating each other with dignity and honor.

JAMES 3:17–18 MSG

Search me, O God, and know my heart; test me and know my anxious
thoughts. Point out anything in me that offends you,
and lead me along the path of everlasting life.

PSALM 139:23–24 NLT

So then, just as you received Christ Jesus as Lord, continue to live in him, rooted and built up in him, strengthened in the faith as you were taught, and overflowing with thankfulness.

COLOSSIANS 2:6–7 NIV

You have made known to me the path of life; you will fill me with joy in your presence, with eternal pleasures at your right hand.
PSALM 16:11 NIV

Always be joyful. Never stop praying. Be thankful in all circumstances,
for this is God's will for you who belong to Christ Jesus.

1 THESSALONIANS 5:16–18 NLT

Trust in the LORD with all thine heart; and lean not unto thine own understanding. In all thy ways acknowledge him, and he shall direct thy paths.

PROVERBS 3:5–6 KJV

I want you woven into a tapestry of love, in touch with everything there
is to know of God. Then you will have minds confident and at rest,
focused on Christ, God's great mystery. All the richest treasures of wisdom
and knowledge are embedded in that mystery and nowhere else.

COLOSSIANS 2:2–3 MSG

Love is patient, love is kind. It does not envy, it does not boast, it is not proud. It is not rude, it is not self-seeking, it is not easily angered, it keeps no record of wrongs. Love does not delight in evil but rejoices with the truth.

1 CORINTHIANS 13:4–6 NIV

Though you have not seen him, you love him; and even though you do not see him now, you believe in him and are filled with an inexpressible and glorious joy, for you are receiving the goal of your faith, the salvation of your souls.

1 PETER 1:8–9 NIV

Praise be to the God and Father of our Lord Jesus Christ! In his great mercy he has given us new birth into a living hope through the resurrection of Jesus Christ from the dead, and into an inheritance that can never perish, spoil or fade—kept in heaven for you, who through faith are shielded by God's power. . . . In this you greatly rejoice.

1 PETER 1:3–6 NIV

So, chosen by God for this new life of love, dress in the wardrobe God picked out for you: compassion, kindness, humility, quiet strength, discipline. Be even-tempered, content with second place, quick to forgive an offense. Forgive as quickly and completely as the Master forgave you. And regardless of what else you put on, wear love. It's your basic, all-purpose garment.

COLOSSIANS 3:12–14 MSG

Surprise us with love at daybreak; then we'll skip and dance all the day long. . . . And let the loveliness of our Lord, our God, rest on us, confirming the work that we do.

PSALM 90:14, 17 MSG

Consider, it pure joy, my brothers, whenever you face trials of many kinds, because you know that the testing of your faith develops perseverance. Perseverance must finish its work so that you may be mature and complete, not lacking anything.

JAMES 1:2–4 NIV

It is absolutely clear that God has called you to a free life. Just make sure that you don't use this freedom as an excuse to do whatever you want to do and destroy your freedom. Rather, use your freedom to serve one another in love; that's how freedom grows.

GALATIANS 5:13 MSG

Have you not known? Have you not heard? The everlasting God, the LORD, the Creator of the ends of the earth, neither faints nor is weary. His understanding is unsearchable.
ISAIAH 40:28 NKJV

What matters is not your outer appearance. . .but your inner disposition.
Cultivate inner beauty, the gentle, gracious kind that God delights in.
1 PETER 3:3–4 MSG

God has given each of you a gift from his great variety of spiritual gifts.
Use them well to serve one another.
1 PETER 4:10 NLT

Don't lose a minute in building on what you've been given, complementing your basic faith with good character, spiritual understanding, alert discipline, passionate patience, reverent wonder, warm friendliness, and generous love, each dimension fitting into and developing the others.

2 PETER 1:5–7 MSG

But what happens when we live God's way? He brings gifts into our lives, much the same way that fruit appears in an orchard—things like affection for others, exuberance about life, serenity.

GALATIANS 5:22 MSG

But when the right time came, God sent his Son, born of a woman, subject to the law. God sent him to buy freedom for us who were slaves to the law, so that he could adopt us as his very own children.

GALATIANS 4:4–5 NLT

Therefore the redeemed of the LORD shall return, and come with singing unto Zion; and everlasting joy shall be upon their head: they shall obtain gladness and joy; and sorrow and mourning shall flee away.

ISAIAH 51:11 KJV

> "If my people, who are called by my name, will humble themselves and pray and seek my face and turn from their wicked ways, then will I hear from heaven and will forgive their sin and will heal their land."
>
> 2 CHRONICLES 7:14 NIV

"*And* why are you worried about clothing? Observe how the lilies of the field grow; they do not toil nor do they spin, yet I say to you that not even Solomon in all his glory clothed himself like one of these."

MATTHEW 6:28–29 NASB

"*God,* having raised up His Servant Jesus, sent Him to bless you, in turning away every one of you from your iniquities."
ACTS 3:26 NKJV

He himself bore our sins in his body on the tree, so that we might die to sins and live for righteousness; by his wounds you have been healed.
1 PETER 2:24 NIV

Those who wait on the LORD shall renew their strength;
they shall mount up with wings like eagles, they shall run
and not be weary, they shall walk and not faint.

ISAIAH 40:31 NKJV

God is our refuge and strength, a very present help in trouble.
PSALM 46:1 NASB

For unto us a child is born, to us a son is given, and the government will be on his shoulders. And he will be called Wonderful Counselor, Mighty God, Everlasting Father, Prince of Peace.
ISAIAH 9:6 NIV

> "*I* do not ask on behalf of these alone, but for those also who believe in Me through their word; that they may all be one; even as You, Father, are in Me and I in You, that they also may be in Us, so that the world may believe that You sent Me."
>
> JOHN 17:20–21 NASB

[The Lord said,] "Every place that the sole
of your foot will tread upon I have given you."
JOSHUA 1:3 NKJV

> *It* is God who works in you to will and
> to act according to his good purpose.
> PHILIPPIANS 2:13 NIV

Yours, O LORD, is the greatness and the power and the glory and the majesty and the splendor, for everything in heaven and earth is yours. Yours, O LORD, is the kingdom; you are exalted as head over all. . . . In your hands are strength and power to exalt and give strength to all.

1 CHRONICLES 29:11–12 NIV

Do you not know that you are the temple of God
and that the Spirit of God dwells in you?
1 Corinthians 3:16 NKJV

"*Haven't* I commanded you? Strength! Courage! Don't be timid; don't get discouraged. GOD, your God, is with you every step you take."

JOSHUA 1:9 MSG

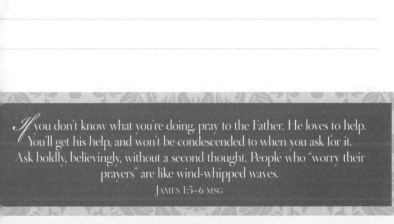

If you don't know what you're doing, pray to the Father. He loves to help. You'll get his help, and won't be condescended to when you ask for it. Ask boldly, believingly, without a second thought. People who "worry their prayers" are like wind-whipped waves.

JAMES 1:5–6 MSG

The Counselor, the Holy Spirit, whom the Father will send in my name, will teach you all things and will remind you of everything I have said to you.

JOHN 14:26 NIV

[God] raised us up with him and seated us with him in the heavenly places in Christ Jesus. . . . For our struggle is not against enemies of blood and flesh, but against the rulers, against the authorities, against the cosmic powers of this present darkness, against the spiritual forces of evil in the heavenly places.

EPHESIANS 2:6; 6:12 NRSV

Trust should be in God, who richly gives us all we need for our enjoyment.
1 TIMOTHY 6:17 NLT

Let the heavens rejoice, let the earth be glad; let them say among the nations, "The LORD reigns!" Let the sea resound, and all that is in it; let the fields be jubilant, and everything in them! Then the trees of the forest will sing, they will sing for joy before the LORD, for he comes to judge the earth. Give thanks to the LORD, for he is good; his love endures forever.

1 CHRONICLES 16:31–34 NIV

Share each other's burdens, and in this way obey the law of Christ.

A cheerful heart is good medicine.
PROVERBS 17:22 NIV

"*To* him the doorkeeper opens, and the sheep hear his voice, and he calls his own sheep by name and leads them out. When he puts forth all his own, he goes ahead of them, and the sheep follow him because they know his voice."

JOHN 10:3–4 NASB

Brethren, I do not regard myself as having laid hold of it yet; but one thing I do: forgetting what lies behind and reaching forward to what lies ahead, I press on toward the goal for the prize of the upward call of God in Christ Jesus.

PHILIPPIANS 3:13–14 NASB

The LORD pours down his blessings.
Our land will yield its bountiful harvest.
PSALM 85:12 NLT

Don't be obsessed with getting more material things.
Be relaxed with what you have. Since God assured us,
"I'll never let you down, never walk off and leave you."
HEBREWS 13:5 MSG

I will say of the LORD, "He is my refuge and my fortress, my God, in whom I trust."
PSALM 91:2 NIV

Through Jesus, therefore, let us continually offer to God a sacrifice of praise—the fruit of lips that confess his name. And do not forget to do good and to share with others, for with such sacrifices God is pleased.

HEBREWS 13:15–16 NIV

Surely goodness and lovingkindness will follow me all the days of my life,
and I will dwell in the house of the LORD forever.

PSALM 23:6 NASB

The deeper your love, the higher it goes; every cloud is
a flag to your faithfulness. Soar high in the skies, O God!
Cover the whole earth with your glory!
PSALM 57:10–11 MSG

It's impossible to please God apart from faith. And why? Because anyone who wants to approach God must believe both that he exists and that he cares enough to respond to those who seek him.

HEBREWS 11:6 MSG

Trust in the LORD with all your heart.
PROVERBS 3:5 NIV

> "*Ah,* Sovereign LORD, you have made the heavens and the earth by your great power and outstretched arm. Nothing is too hard for you."
> JEREMIAH 32:17 NIV

"*Listen* to me. . .you whom I have upheld since you were conceived, and have carried since your birth. Even to your old age and gray hairs I am he, I am he who will sustain you. I have made you and I will carry you."

ISAIAH 46:3–4 NIV

> "*Be* still, and know that I am God; I will be exalted among the nations, I will be exalted in the earth."
>
> PSALM 46:10 NIV

May the God of hope fill you with all joy and peace as you trust in him,
so that you may overflow with hope.

ROMANS 15:13 NIV

For great is your love, higher than the heavens; your faithfulness reaches to the skies. Be exalted, O God, above the heavens, and let your glory be over all the earth.

PSALM 108:4–5 NIV

....

....

....

....

....

....

....

....

....

....

....

....

....

The moon marks off the seasons, and the sun knows when to go down. . . .
How many are your works, O LORD! In wisdom you made them all.
PSALM 104:19, 24 NIV

God is sheer mercy and grace; not easily angered, he's rich in love. . . .
As high as heaven is over the earth, so strong is his love to those who fear him.
And as far as sunrise is from sunset, he has separated us from our sins.

PSALM 103:8, 11–12 MSG

One thing I ask of the LORD, this is what I seek: that I may dwell in the house of the LORD all the days of my life, to gaze upon the beauty of the LORD and to seek him in his temple.

PSALM 27:4 NIV

O LORD, you have searched me and you know me. You know when I sit and when I rise; you perceive my thoughts from afar. You discern my going out and my lying down; you are familiar with all my ways.

PSALM 139:1–3 NIV

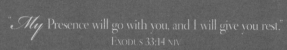

"*My* Presence will go with you, and I will give you rest."
EXODUS 33:14 NIV

O the depth of the riches and wisdom and knowledge of God!
How unsearchable are his judgments and how inscrutable his ways!
ROMANS 11:33 NRSV

Seek the Lord and his strength, seek his presence continually.
Remember the wonderful works he has done, his miracles.
1 CHRONICLES 16:11–12 NRSV

The LORD will guide you always; he will satisfy your needs in
a sun-scorched land. . . . You will be like a well-watered garden,
like a spring whose waters never fail.

ISAIAH 58:11 NIV

"*Assuredly*, I say to you, if you have faith as a mustard seed, you will
say to this mountain, 'Move from here to there,' and it will move;
and nothing will be impossible for you."
MATTHEW 17:20 NKJV

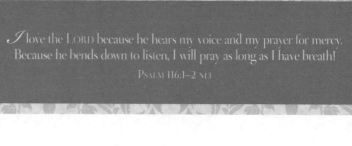

I love the LORD because he hears my voice and my prayer for mercy.
Because he bends down to listen, I will pray as long as I have breath!

PSALM 116:1–2 NLT

Cast all your anxiety on him because he cares for you.
1 PETER 5:7 NIV

God's love is meteoric, his loyalty astronomic, his purpose titanic,
his verdicts oceanic. Yet in his largeness nothing gets lost.

PSALM 36:5–6 MSG

Go, eat your food with gladness, and drink your wine with a joyful heart,
for it is now that God favors what you do.

ECCLESIASTES 9:7 NIV

Delight yourself in the LORD and
he will give you the desires of your heart.
PSALM 37:4 NIV

The steadfast love of the Lord never ceases, his mercies never come to an end; they are new every morning; great is your faithfulness.

LAMENTATIONS 3:22–23 NRSV

The life appeared; we have seen it and testify to it, and we proclaim to you the eternal life, which was with the Father and has appeared to us.

1 JOHN 1:2 NIV

"*My* heart rejoices in the LORD!"
1 SAMUEL 2:1 NLT

No one has ever seen God; but if we love one another,
God lives in us and his love is made complete in us.
1 JOHN 4:12 NIV

Folly is joy to him who is destitute of discernment,
but a man of understanding walks uprightly.
PROVERBS 15:21 NKJV

May he give you the desire of your heart and make all your plans succeed.
We will shout for joy when you are victorious and will lift up our banners in
the name of our God.

PSALM 20:4–5 NIV

Do not fear, for I am with you; do not be dismayed,
for I am your God. I will strengthen you and help you;
I will uphold you with my righteous right hand.

ISAIAH 41:10 NIV

Give thanks unto the LORD, call upon his name,
make known his deeds among the people.

1 CHRONICLES 16:8 KJV

Everything God created is good, and to be received with thanks.
1 TIMOTHY 4:4 MSG

Let the peace of Christ rule in your hearts, since as members of one body
you were called to peace. And be thankful.

COLOSSIANS 3:15 NIV

Blessed is the man who perseveres under trial,
because when he has stood the test, he will receive the crown
of life that God has promised to those who love him.

JAMES 1:12 NIV

But by the grace of God I am what I am.
1 CORINTHIANS 15:10 KJV

> *Give* thanks to the LORD, for he is good. His love endures forever.
> Give thanks to the God of gods. His love endures forever. Give thanks
> to the Lord of lords: his love endures forever. To him who alone
> does great wonders, his love endures forever.
>
> PSALM 136:1–4 NIV

You changed my sorrow into dancing.
You took away my clothes of sadness, and clothed me in happiness.
Psalm 30:11 NCV

But rejoice that you participate in the sufferings of Christ,
so that you may be overjoyed when his glory is revealed.
1 PETER 4:13 NIV

Beloved, let us love one another: for love is of God;
and every one that loveth is born of God, and knoweth God.
1 JOHN 4:7 KJV

With joy you will drink deeply from the fountain of salvation!
Isaiah 12:3 NLT

I have learned to be content whatever the circumstances. I know what it is to be in need, and I know what it is to have plenty. I have learned the secret of being content in any and every situation, whether well fed or hungry, whether living in plenty or in want.

PHILIPPIANS 4:11–12 NIV

Restore unto me the joy of thy salvation;
and uphold me with thy free spirit.
PSALM 51:12 KJV

My aim is to raise hopes by pointing the way to life without end.
This is the life God promised long ago—and he doesn't break promises!
TITUS 1:2 MSG

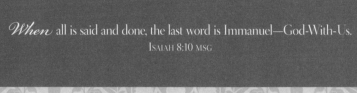

When all is said and done, the last word is Immanuel—God-With-Us.
ISAIAH 8:10 MSG

The heavens declare the glory of God; the skies proclaim the work of his hands. Day after day they pour forth speech; night after night they display knowledge.

PSALM 19:1–2 NIV

Many, O LORD my God, are the wonders you have done....
Were I to speak and tell of them, they would be too many to declare.
PSALM 40:5 NIV

There is a time for everything. . .a time to weep and a time to laugh.
ECCLESIASTES 3:1, 4 NIV

For GOD is sheer beauty, all-generous in love, loyal always and ever.

PSALM 100:5 MSG

There is more joy in heaven over one lost sinner who repents
and returns to God than over ninety-nine others who are
righteous and haven't strayed away!

LUKE 15:7 NLT

We know that suffering produces perseverance;
perseverance, character; and character, hope.
ROMANS 5:3–4 NIV

> "*If* God gives such attention to the appearance of wildflowers—most of which are never even seen—don't you think he'll attend to you, take pride in you, do his best for you?"
>
> MATTHEW 6:30 MSG

You know with all your heart and soul that not one of all the good promises the LORD your God gave you has failed. Every promise has been fulfilled.

JOSHUA 23:14 NIV

Let us fix our eyes on Jesus, the author and perfecter of our faith.
HEBREWS 12:2 NIV

As we have opportunity, let us do good to all people.
GALATIANS 6:10 NIV

That Christ may dwell in your hearts by faith; that ye, being rooted and grounded in love, may be able to comprehend with all saints what is the breadth, and length, and depth, and height; and to know the love of Christ, which passeth knowledge, that ye might be filled with all the fulness of God.

EPHESIANS 3:17–19 KJV

May our Lord Jesus Christ. . .encourage your hearts
and strengthen you in every good deed and word.
2 THESSALONIANS 2:16–17 NIV

Friends love through all kinds of weather.
PROVERBS 17:17 MSG

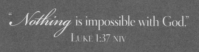
"*Nothing* is impossible with God."
LUKE 1:37 NIV

A cheerful heart fills the day with song.
PROVERBS 15:15 MSG

Commit to the LORD whatever you do, and your plans will succeed.
PROVERBS 16:3 NIV

Wisdom will enter your heart,
and knowledge will be pleasant to your soul.
PROVERBS 2:10 NIV

Charity yields high returns.
ECCLESIASTES 11:1 MSG

"*You* will rejoice, and no one will take away your joy."
JOHN 16:22 NIV

Be strong in the grace that is in Christ Jesus.
2 TIMOTHY 2:1 NIV

Friends come and friends go, but a true friend sticks by you like family.
PROVERBS 18:24 MSG

Bless the LORD, O my soul, and forget not all his benefits.

PSALM 103:2 KJV

I will sing for joy in God, explode in praise from deep in my soul! . . .
For as the earth bursts with spring wildflowers, and as a garden cascades with
blossoms, so the Master, God, brings righteousness into full bloom.

Isaiah 61:10–11 MSG

Even though on the outside it often looks like things are falling apart on us, on the inside, where God is making new life, not a day goes by without his unfolding grace.

2 CORINTHIANS 4:16 MSG

God is able to make all grace abound to you, so that in all things at all times, having all that you need, you will abound in every good work.

2 CORINTHIANS 9:8 NIV

Yet I will rejoice in the LORD, I will be joyful in God my Savior.

HABAKKUK 3:18 NIV

Blessed be the Lord—day after day he carries us along.
PSALM 68:19 MSG

Be kind to one another, tender-hearted, forgiving each other,
just as God in Christ also has forgiven you.

EPHESIANS 4:32 NASB

God has given us different gifts for doing certain things well. . . .
If your gift is serving others, serve them well. . . . And if you have a gift
for showing kindness to others, do it gladly.

ROMANS 12:6–8 NLT